Christmas
2012
Presented To:

My Pal, Val

From:

Your Forever Friend,
Dianne

Freeman-Smith, a division of Worthy Media, Inc.
134 Franklin Road, Suite 200, Brentwood, Tennessee 37027

The quoted ideas expressed in this book (but not Scripture verses) are not, in all cases, exact quotations, as some have been edited for clarity and brevity. In all cases, the author has attempted to maintain the speaker's original intent. In some cases, quoted material for this book was obtained from secondary sources, primarily print media. While every effort was made to ensure the accuracy of these sources, the accuracy cannot be guaranteed. For additions, deletions, corrections, or clarifications in future editions of this text, please write Freeman-Smith.

Scripture quotations are taken from:

The Holy Bible, King James Version (KJV)

The Holy Bible, New King James Version (NKJV) Copyright © 1982 by Thomas Nelson, Inc. Used by permission.

The Holman Christian Standard Bible™ (HCSB) Copyright © 1999, 2000, 2001 by Holman Bible Publishers. Used by permission.

Cover Design by Scott Williams/Richmond & Williams
Page Layout by Bart Dawson

ISBN 978-1-60587-377-0

1 2 3 4 5—RRD—16 15 14 13 12

Printed in China

CELEBRATE THE JOY OF CHRISTMAS!

PETALS OF Joy

Table of Contents

But the angel said to them,
"Do not be afraid, for you see,
I announce to you good news
of great joy that will be for
all the people: because today
in the city of David
was born for you a Savior,
who is Christ the Lord."

LUKE 2:10-11 HCSB

Introduction

Christmas is intended to be a joyful season, a time when we gather together to exchange gifts and celebrate God's ultimate gift to the world. Yet sometimes, amid the crush of holiday obligations, we may be tempted to forget, at least temporarily, the One whose birth we celebrate.

This book is intended to remind family members of all ages that God's promises are everlasting, that His joy is available to all, and that His grace is given freely to those who accept His Son into their hearts.

The Christmas holidays are, of course, a time when Christians the world over celebrate the birth of Jesus. Have you made the choice to rejoice? Are you spreading petals of joy wherever you go? Are you slowing down long enough to praise your Creator for His infinite blessings and His infinite love? Hopefully so. After all, this holiday season, like each one before it, is a gift from God, a gift to be savored and celebrated. And, the best day to begin that celebration is the current one.

CHAPTER I

Christmas Is Joy

The Christmas season is a time for joy and celebration. In the hamlet of Bethlehem, God gave the world a priceless gift: the Christ child. We, as believers, can rejoice: God, through His Son, has offered spiritual abundance and salvation to the world.

During our earthly existence, of course, we will all have trials and troubles—but as believers we are secure. God has promised us peace, joy, and eternal life. So, as we join in the celebrations of this sacred holiday, let us rejoice in God's most glorious gift: a baby born in a manger, a baby who forever changed the world. And then, with hope in our hearts and praise on our lips, let the celebration begin!

Joyful, joyful, we adore thee,
God of glory, Lord of love.
Hearts unfold like flowers before thee;
opening to the sun above.

HENRY VAN DYKE

Rejoice, that the immortal God is born,
so that mortal man may live in eternity.

JAN HUS

Christ and joy go together.

E. STANLEY JONES

Joy is the serious business of heaven.

C. S. LEWIS

Joy comes not from what we have
but from what we are.

C. H. SPURGEON

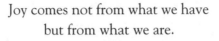

Happiness is the by-product of a life that is lived
in the will of God. When we humbly serve others,
walk in God's path of holiness, and do what
He tells us, then we will enjoy happiness.

WARREN WIERSBE

*Rejoice in the Lord, you righteous ones;
praise from the upright is beautiful.*

PSALM 33:1 HCSB

God can take any man and
put the miracle of His joy into him.

OSWALD CHAMBERS

❦

When we bring sunshine into the lives of others,
we're warmed by it ourselves.
When we spill a little happiness, it splashes on us.

BARBARA JOHNSON

❦

Our God is so wonderfully good, and lovely,
and blessed in every way that
the mere fact of belonging to Him is enough
for an untellable fullness of joy!

HANNAH WHITALL SMITH

❦

Until now you have asked for nothing in My name.
Ask and you will receive,
that your joy may be complete.

JOHN 16:24 HCSB

Where the soul is full of peace and joy,
outward surroundings and circumstances
are of comparatively little account.

HANNAH WHITALL SMITH

⌒⌒⌒

True happiness and contentment cannot come
from the things of this world. The blessedness of
true joy is a free gift that comes only from
our Lord and Savior, Jesus Christ.

DENNIS SWANBERG

⌒⌒⌒

This is the happy life: to rejoice to Thee, of Thee,
for Thee; this it is, and there is no other.

ST. AUGUSTINE

⌒⌒⌒

Rejoice always, pray without ceasing,
in everything give thanks;
for this is the will of God in Christ Jesus for you.

1 THESSALONIANS 5:16-18 NKJV

Joy is the direct result of having God's perspective
on our daily lives and the effect of loving
our Lord enough to obey His commands
and trust His promises.

BILL BRIGHT

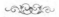

Joy cannot be pursued. It comes from within.
It is a state of being. It does not depend on
circumstances, but triumphs over circumstances.
It produces a gentleness of spirit
and a magnetic personality.

BILLY GRAHAM

*Rejoice in the Lord always.
I will say it again: Rejoice!*
PHILIPPIANS 4:4 HCSB

When I think of
Christmas Eves, Christmas
feasts, Christmas songs, and
Christmas stories, I know it
was not a short and transient
gladness. It was—and is—
a joy unspeakable
and full of glory.

—

GORRIE TEN BOOM

*This is the day
the Lord has made;
we will rejoice
and be glad in it.*

—

PSALM 118:24 NKJV

CHAPTER 2

A Child Is Born

The Christmas story began in the little town of Bethlehem, in a manger. It was there, in the most humble of circumstances, that God fulfilled His Old Testament promise by offering salvation to the world. Not far from that manger, shepherds were tending their flock:

And it came to pass in those days that a decree went out from Caesar Augustus that all the world should be registered. This census first took place while Quirinius was governing Syria. So all went to be registered, everyone to his own city. Joseph also went up from Galilee, out of the city of Nazareth, into Judea, to the city of David, which is called Bethlehem, because he was of the house and lineage of David, to be registered with Mary, his betrothed wife, who was with child. So it was, that while they were there, the days were completed for her to be delivered. And she brought forth her firstborn Son, and wrapped Him in swaddling cloths, and laid

Him in a manger, because there was no room for them in the inn. Now there were in the same country shepherds living out in the fields, keeping watch over their flock by night. And behold, an angel of the Lord stood before them, and the glory of the Lord shone around them, and they were greatly afraid. Then the angel said to them, "Do not be afraid, for behold, I bring you good tidings of great joy which will be to all people. For there is born to you this day in the city of David a Savior, who is Christ the Lord. And this will be the sign to you: You will find a Babe wrapped in swaddling cloths, lying in a manger." And suddenly there was with the angel a multitude of the heavenly host praising God and saying: "Glory to God in the highest, And on earth peace, goodwill toward men!"

Luke 2:1-14 NKJV

The Christ child changed the world forever, and He can do the same for us. On this Christmas day, we, like the shepherds of old, are called to celebrate the birth of the baby named Jesus. May we, like those shepherds, leave our fields—wherever they may be—and pause to worship God's priceless Christmas gift: His Son.

*The birth of Jesus
is the sunrise in the Bible.*

—

HENRY VAN DYKE

Jesus Christ was born into this world,
not from it.

OSWALD CHAMBERS

The whole meaning of Christmas can be
summed up in the miracle of Christ's birth.

ARTHUR BRYANT

All the earth shall worship You
And sing praises to You;
They shall sing praises to Your name.

PSALM 66:4 NKJV

Infinite, and an infant.
Eternal, and yet born of a woman.
Heir of all things, yet the carpenter's son.

C. H. SPURGEON

The Son of God became man to enable men
to become sons of God.

C. S. LEWIS

For God did not send His Son into the world
that He might judge the world,
but that the world might be saved through Him.

JOHN 3:17 HCSB

Jesus Christ founded His Kingdom
on the weakest link of all:
a Baby.

OSWALD CHAMBERS

The old message "For unto you is born this day
in the city of David a Savior which is
Christ the Lord" is still the heart of Christmas.

PETER MARSHALL

For the Son of Man has come to save the lost.

MATTHEW 18:11 HCSB

All praise to Thee, Eternal Lord,
clothed in a garb of flesh and blood,
choosing a manger for a throne.

MARTIN LUTHER

The manger is a symbol of what can happen
when Jesus Christ resides inside us.
The ordinary suddenly becomes extraordinary.

BILL HYBELS

The magic message of Christmas is that
God gave us so much more
than we can possibly give back!

NORMAN VINCENT PEALE

Even before God created the heavens
and the earth, He knew you and me,
and He chose us! You and I were born
because it was God's good pleasure.

KAY ARTHUR

The grace of God is infinite and eternal.
As it had no beginning, so it can have no end,
and being an attribute of God,
it is as boundless as infinitude.

A. W. TOZER

If you have a true faith that Christ is your Savior,
then at once you have a gracious God,
for faith leads you in and opens up God's heart
and will, that you should see
pure grace and overflowing love.

MARTIN LUTHER

For I am persuaded that
neither death nor life, nor angels
nor rulers, nor things present,
nor things to come, nor powers,
nor height, nor depth, nor any
other created thing will have
the power to separate us from
the love of God that is in
Christ Jesus our Lord!

—

ROMANS 8:38–39 HCSB

Go tell it on the mountain,
over the hills and everywhere.
Go tell it on the mountain,
that Jesus Christ is born!

—

TRADITIONAL AMERICAN SPIRITUAL

CHAPTER 3

The Promise of Joy

*I have spoken these things to you so that My joy
may be in you and your joy may be complete.*
JOHN 15:11 HCSB

The prophecies of the Old Testament foretell the promise of Christmas: "For a child will be born for us, a son will be given to us, and the government will be on His shoulders. He will be named Wonderful Counselor, Mighty God, Eternal Father, Prince of Peace" (Isaiah 9:6 HCSB). In Bethlehem God fulfilled His promise on that joyful night when a babe was born in a manger. And every year at Christmastime, we celebrate the birth of the Christ child, God's priceless gift to the world.

Christ made it clear: He intends that His joy should become our joy. Yet sometimes, amid the inevitable hustle and bustle of life here on earth, we can forfeit—albeit temporarily—the joy of Christ as we wrestle with the challenges of daily living.

Jonathan Edwards, the 18th-century American clergyman, observed, "Christ is not only a remedy for your weariness and trouble, but he will give you an abundance of the contrary: joy and delight. They who come to Christ do not only come to a resting-place after they have been wandering in a wilderness, but they come to a banqueting-house where they may rest, and where they may feast. They may cease from their former troubles and toils, and they may enter upon a course of delights and spiritual joys."

This year's Christmas celebration provides yet another opportunity to praise God for His infinite love and for His incalculable gifts. May you and yours celebrate both.

Claim the joy that is yours. Pray. And know that your joy is used by God to reach others.

KAY ARTHUR

Jesus came into the world so we could know,
once and for all, that God is concerned about
the way we live, the way we believe,
and the way we die.

BILLY GRAHAM

The Son of God does not want to be seen and
found in heaven. Therefore he descended from
heaven to this earth and came to us in our flesh.

MARTIN LUTHER

Jesus is the personal approach from the unseen God
coming so near that he becomes inescapable.
You don't have to find him—
you just have to consent to be found.

E. STANLEY JONES

What a paradox that a babe in
a manger should be called mighty!
Yet even as a babe, Jesus Christ
was the center of power.
His birth affected the heavens and
caused a dazzling star to appear.
Midnight became midday
as the glory of the Lord
appeared to men.

—

WARREN WIERSBE

Christmas means the beginning of Christianity—
and a second chance for the world.

PETER MARSHALL

If we could condense all the truths
of Christmas into only three words,
these would be the words:
"God with us."

JOHN MACARTHUR

The miracle of Christmas is not on 34th Street;
it's in Bethlehem.

RICK WARREN

Tell me the story of Jesus.
Write on my heart every word.
Tell me the story most precious,
sweetest that ever was heard.

—

FANNY CROSBY

The Word had become flesh, a real human baby.
He had not ceased to be God.
He was no less God then than before,
but He had begun to be man. He was not now
God minus some elements of His deity
but God plus all that He had made His own
by taking manhood to himself.

J. I. PACKER

The crucial question for each of us is this:
What do you think of Jesus, and do you yet
have a personal acquaintance with Him?

HANNAH WHITALL SMITH

Just as Our Lord came into human history from
outside, so He must come into me from outside.
Have I allowed my personal human life
to become a "Bethlehem" for the Son of God?

OSWALD CHAMBERS

On Christmas Day two thousand years ago,
the birth of a tiny baby
in an obscure village in the Middle East was
God's supreme triumph of good over evil.

CHARLES COLSON

Jesus—the standard of measurement,
the scale of weights, the test of character
for the whole moral universe.

R. G. LEE

Jesus was the perfect reflection of God's nature
in every situation He encountered
during His time here on earth.

BILL HYBELS

Jesus Christ is the same yesterday,
today, and forever.

HEBREWS 13:8 HCSB

Begin to know Him now,
and finish never.

OSWALD CHAMBERS

So Jesus came, stripping himself of everything
as he came—omnipotence, omniscience,
omnipresence—everything except love.
"He emptied himself" (Philippians 2:7),
emptied himself of everything except love.
Love—his only protection,
his only weapon, his only method.

E. STANLEY JONES

He loved us not because we're lovable,
but because He is love.

C. S. LEWIS

Being a Christian is more than
just an instantaneous conversion;
it is like a daily process whereby you grow
to be more and more like Christ.

BILLY GRAHAM

Then let every heart keep
Christmas within.
Christ's pity for sorrow,
Christ's hatred for sin,
Christ's care for the weakest,
Christ's courage for right,
Everywhere, everywhere,
Christmas tonight!

—

PHILLIPS BROOKS

My lips will shout for joy
when I sing praise to You.

PSALM 71:23 HCSB

Shout to the Lord, all the earth;
be jubilant, shout for joy, and sing.

PSALM 98:4 HCSB

I will thank the Lord with all my heart;
I will declare all Your wonderful works.
I will rejoice and boast about You;
I will sing about Your name, Most High.

PSALM 9:1-2 HCSB

CHAPTER 4

Christmas Is . . .

Christmas is the glorious day on which we celebrate that pivotal event in human history, the birth of Christ. No amount of commercialism or fanfare should obscure the fact that Christmastime is the annual birthday celebration for the Christian faith, a time for believers everywhere to rejoice, to pray, and to give thanks for God's greatest treasure: His Son.

Billy Graham observed, "Christmas is the celebration of the event that set Heaven to singing, an event that gave the stars of the night sky a new brilliance." As we prepare for the busy days that lead up to Christmas, it is appropriate that we remain mindful of the real reason for the holiday season by offering our prayers and our praise to the One whose birth we celebrate.

*Christmas is about a baby,
born in a stable,
who changed the world
forever.*

—

JOHN MAXWELL

*Christmas is the day
that holds all time together.*

—

ALEXANDER SMITH

The Christmas story gives its triumphant answer:
"Be not afraid."

KARL BARTH

❦

The Christmas spirit—love—
changes hearts and lives.

PAT BOONE

❦

If Christmas is about anything,
Christmas is the story of God changing worlds
and putting limitations upon Himself.
It's the story of a baby born in Bethlehem,
who was much more powerful than
the Roman Empire that existed that day.

JOHN MAXWELL

The Christmas message is that there is hope for humanity, hope of pardon, hope of peace with God, hope of glory.

J. I. PACKER

Christmas, like God,
is timeless and eternal.

DALE EVANS

Christmas is not just a day of the year.
It is also—and more importantly—
a condition of the heart.

MARIE T. FREEMAN

Christmas, my child,
is love in action.
Every time we love,
every time we give,
it's Christmas.

—

DALE EVANS

Then Jesus spoke to them again:
"I am the light of the world.
Anyone who follows Me
will never walk in the darkness,
but will have the light of life."

—

JOHN 8:12 HCSB

CHAPTER 5

Worshipping
the Christ Child

Nothing should obscure the fact that Christmastime is the annual birthday celebration of the Christian faith. Christmas day is, above all else, a religious holiday—a time for Christians everywhere to rejoice, to pray, and to worship God.

The 25th day of December, like every other day of the year, provides countless opportunities to put God where He belongs: at the center of our lives. When we do so, we are blessed.

During this holiday season, it is proper that we keep our eyes, our voices, and our hearts lifted upward as we offer profound thanksgiving to God through our worship and our praise.

On Christmas, we celebrate the day when
the Son of God became the Son of Man.
We celebrate the day when
the Son of the Highest stooped to the lowest,
a day when the King
of Glory shed his splendor and
became poor that we,
through his poverty, might be rich.

ARTHUR M. BRAZIER

When God is at the center of your life,
you worship.
When he's not, you worry.

RICK WARREN

Praise Him! Praise Him!
Tell of His excellent greatness.
Praise Him! Praise Him!
Ever in joyful song!

FANNY CROSBY

In the sanctuary, we discover beauty:
the beauty of His presence.

KAY ARTHUR

*I rejoiced with those who said to me,
"Let us go to the house of the Lord."*

PSALM 122:1 HCSB

51

Praise and thank God for who He is
and for what He has done for you.

<small>BILLY GRAHAM</small>

❧⟡❧

The fact that we were created to enjoy God
and to worship him forever
is etched upon our souls.

<small>JIM CYMBALA</small>

❧⟡❧

It is only with gratitude
that life becomes rich.

<small>DIETRICH BONHOEFFER</small>

The deepest level of worship is praising God in spite of pain, thanking God during a trial, trusting him when tempted, surrendering while suffering, and loving him when he seems distant.

RICK WARREN

The ability to rejoice in any situation is a sign of spiritual maturity.

BILLY GRAHAM

Praise the Lord!
Oh, give thanks to the Lord, for He is good!
For His mercy endures forever.

PSALM 106:1 NKJV

53

*But an hour is coming, and is now here, when the true
worshipers will worship the Father in spirit and truth.
Yes, the Father wants such people to worship Him.
God is Spirit, and those who worship Him
must worship in spirit and truth.*

JOHN 4:23-24 HCSB

*I am the bread of life, Jesus told them.
"No one who comes to Me will ever be hungry,
and no one who believes in Me
will ever be thirsty again."*

JOHN 6:35 HCSB

There's no better time than Christmas to become
the kind of seeker the wise men embodied.
Wise people still seek Christ.

RICK WARREN

He is the image of the invisible God,
the firstborn over all creation; because by Him
everything was created, in heaven and on earth,
the visible and the invisible, whether thrones or
dominions or rulers or authorities—
all things have been created through Him and for Him.

COLOSSIANS 1:15-16 HCSB

For where two or three are gathered together
in My name, I am there among them.

MATTHEW 18:20 HCSB

It is impossible to worship God
and remain unchanged.

HENRY BLACKABY

Worship is not taught from the pulpit.
It must be learned in the heart.

JIM ELLIOT

Worship is a voluntary act of gratitude
offered by the saved to the Savior,
by the healed to the Healer,
by the delivered to the Deliverer.

MAX LUCADO

*Therefore, through Him let us continually offer up
to God a sacrifice of praise, that is,
the fruit of our lips that confess His name.*

HEBREWS 13:15 HCSB

Worship is your spirit
responding to God's Spirit.

RICK WARREN

Worship and worry cannot live in the same heart;
they are mutually exclusive.

RUTH BELL GRAHAM

It's our privilege to not only raise our hands in
worship but also to combine the visible with
the invisible in a rising stream of praise and
adoration sent directly to our Father.

SHIRLEY DOBSON

Spiritual worship comes from
our very core and is fueled by
an awesome reverence and desire for God.

BETH MOORE

Nothing we do is more powerful or
more life-changing than praising God.

STORMIE OMARTIAN

Our God is the sovereign Creator of the universe!
He loves us as His own children and has
provided every good thing we have;
He is worthy of our praise every moment.

SHIRLEY DOBSON

It's the definition of worship:
A hungry heart finding the Father's feast.
A searching soul finding the Father's face.
A wandering pilgrim spotting the Father's house.
Finding God. Finding God seeking us.
This is worship. This is a worshiper.

MAX LUCADO

Worship is wonder, love, and praise.
Not only does it cause us to contemplate and
appreciate our holy God, but it gives us vitality,
vigor, and a desire to obey Him.

FRANKLIN GRAHAM

In commanding us to glorify Him,
God is inviting us to enjoy Him.

C. S. LEWIS

*The time for universal praise
is sure to come some day.
Let us begin
to do our part now.*

—

HANNAH WHITALL SMITH

CHAPTER 6

Sharing Christ's Gifts

The old familiar hymn begins, "What a friend we have in Jesus . . ." No truer words were ever penned. Christ showed enduring love by willingly sacrificing His own life so that we might have eternal life. As believers, we are blessed beyond measure—and God calls upon us to share our blessings.

Christmas is the season for giving, but gift-giving need not be synonymous with commercialism. The holiday season is the perfect time to share spiritual gifts as well as material ones. Spiritual gifts, of course, should take priority, but we must also give freely of our possessions, especially to those in need.

The words of Jesus are unambiguous: "Freely you have received, freely give" (Matthew 10:8 NKJV). May this holiday season, and every one hereafter, be a time when we, as followers of Christ, show our love for Him through the generosity that we show to others.

Christmas is based on
an exchange of gifts;
the gift of God to man,
His Son;
and the gift of man to God,
when we first give
ourselves to God.

—

VANCE HAVNER

This is Christmas, the real meaning of it:
God loving, searching, giving Himself to us;
man needing, receiving, giving himself to God.
Redemption's glorious exchange of gifts,
without which we cannot live, without which
we cannot give to those we love anything of lasting
value. This is the meaning of Christmas,
the wonder and the glory of it.

RUTH BELL GRAHAM

The righteous give and don't hold back.

PROVERBS 21:26 HCSB

Let us give according to our incomes,
lest God make our incomes match our gifts.

PETER MARSHALL

Let us remember that the Christmas heart
is a giving heart, a wide-open heart that thinks
of others first. The birth of the baby Jesus
stands as the most significant event in all history
because it has meant the pouring into
a sick world of the healing medicine of love
which has transformed all manner of hearts
for almost two thousand years.

GEORGE MATTHEW ADAMS

To celebrate the heart of Christmas is to forget
ourselves in the service of others.

HENRY C. LINK

Whatever you did for one of the least of these
brothers of Mine, you did for Me

MATTHEW 25:40 HCSB

*So let each one give
as he purposes in his heart,
not grudgingly or of necessity;
for God loves a cheerful giver.*

—

2 CORINTHIANS 9:7 NKJV

*It is the duty of
every Christian
to be Christ
to his neighbor.*

—

MARTIN LUTHER

Generosity is changing one's focus
from self to others.

JOHN MAXWELL

A happy spirit takes the grind out of giving.
The grease of gusto
frees the gears of generosity.

CHARLES SWINDOLL

The measure of a life, after all,
is not its duration but its donation.

CORRIE TEN BOOM

PETALS OF *Joy*

Giving to God and, in His name, to others,
is not something that we do;
it the result of what we are.

WARREN WIERSBE

*And may the Lord make you increase
and abound in love to one another and to all.*

1 THESSALONIANS 3:12 NKJV

Selfishness is as far from Christianity
as darkness is from light.

C. H. SPURGEON

Jesus had a loving heart.
If he dwells within us,
hatred and bitterness
will never rule us.

—

BILLY GRAHAM

*Christmas is most truly
Christmas when we celebrate it
by giving the light of love
to those who need it most.*

—

RUTH CARTER STAPLETON

CHAPTER 7

Joyful Songs of Celebration and Praise

As we grow older many things about Christmas change. But some things remain the same, including the songs that we sing. When it comes to Yuletide fare, our musical tastes are slow to change. Thank goodness.

The songs of Christmas, especially our favorite hymns, rank among the most beloved compositions ever penned. On the pages that follow, we celebrate a few of the songs we sing at Christmastime: may these holiday classics remain unchanged forever.

Away in a Manger

Away in a manger,
no crib for a bed,
The little Lord Jesus
lay down his sweet head.
The stars in the sky
looked down where he lay,
The little Lord Jesus,
asleep on the hay.

The cattle are lowing,
the baby awakes,
But little Lord Jesus,
no crying he makes.
I love Thee, Lord Jesus!
Look down from the sky,
And stay by my cradle
till morning is nigh.

Be near me, Lord Jesus,
I ask Thee to stay
Close by me forever,
and love me, I pray.
Bless all the dear children
in thy tender care,
And take us to heaven,
to live with Thee there.

—

ANONYMOUS

God Rest You Merry Gentlemen

God rest you merry, gentlemen,
Let nothing you dismay,
Remember Christ our Savior
Was born on Christmas Day,
To save us all from Satan's pow'r
When we were gone astray;
O tidings of comfort and joy,
comfort and joy,
O tidings of comfort and joy.

From God our heavenly Father,
A blessed angel came.
And unto certain shepherds,
Brought tidings of the same;
How that in Bethlehem was born
The Son of God by name;
O tidings of comfort and joy,
comfort and joy,
O tidings of comfort and joy.

—

TRADITIONAL 17TH-CENTURY ENGLISH CAROL

It Came Upon the Midnight Clear

It came upon the midnight clear,
That glorious song of old,
From angels bending near the earth,
To touch their harps of gold.
Peace on the earth, goodwill to men,
From heav'n's all gracious king,
The world in solemn stillness lay
To hear the angels sing.

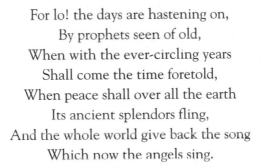

For lo! the days are hastening on,
By prophets seen of old,
When with the ever-circling years
Shall come the time foretold,
When peace shall over all the earth
Its ancient splendors fling,
And the whole world give back the song
Which now the angels sing.

—

EDMUND SEARS, 1850

Silent Night

Silent Night! Holy Night!
All is calm, all is bright.
Round yon virgin mother and child!
Holy infant so tender and mild,
Sleep in heavenly peace,
sleep in heavenly peace.

Silent Night! Holy Night!
Shepherds quake at the sight!
Glories stream from heaven afar,
Heavenly hosts sing Alleluia!
Christ the Savior is born!
Christ the Savior is born!

Silent Night! Holy Night!
Son of God, love's pure light;
Radiant beams from Thy holy face,
With the dawn of redeeming grace,
Jesus Lord, at Thy birth,
Jesus Lord, at Thy birth.

—

FATHER JOSEPH MOHR, 1818

Joy to the World

Joy to the world! the Lord is come:
Let earth receive her King;
Let every heart prepare him room,
And heaven and nature sing.
And heaven and nature sing.
And heaven, and heaven, and nature sing.

Joy to the world! the Saviour reigns:
Let men their songs employ;
While fields and floods, rocks, hills, and plains
Repeat the sounding joy.
Repeat the sounding joy.
Repeat, repeat the sounding joy.

He rules the world with truth and grace,
And makes the nations prove
The glories of his righteousness,
And wonders of his love.
And wonders of his love.
And wonders, wonders of his love.

WORDS BY ISAAC WATTS (1674-1748)
MUSIC BY LOWELL MASON (1792-1872)

The First Noel

The first Noel the angel did say
Was to certain poor shepherds
in fields as they lay;
In fields as they lay, keeping their sheep,
On a cold winter's night that was so deep.

Noel, Noel, Noel, Noel,
Born is the King of Israel.

They looked up and saw a star
Shining in the east beyond them far,
And to the earth it gave great light,
And so it continued both day and night.

Noel, Noel, Noel, Noel,
Born is the King of Israel.

Then entered in those wise men three
Full reverently upon their knee,
And offered there in his presence
Their gold, and myrrh, and frankincense.

Noel, Noel, Noel, Noel,
Born is the King of Israel.

Then let us all with one accord
Sing praises to our heavenly Lord;
That hath made heaven and earth of naught,
And with his blood mankind hath bought.

—

TRADITIONAL ENGLISH CAROL

O Little Town of Bethlehem

O little town of Bethlehem,
How still we see thee lie,
Above thy deep and dreamless sleep,
The silent stars go by;
Yet in thy dark streets shineth
The everlasting Light,
The hopes and fears of all the years
Are met in thee tonight.

For Christ is born of Mary,
And gathered all above,
While mortals sleep, the angels keep
Their watch of wondering love.
O morning stars, together
Proclaim the holy birth!
And praises sing to God the King,
And peace to men on earth.

How silently, how silently,
The wondrous gift is giv'n!
So God imparts to human hearts
The blessings of His heav'n.
No ear may hear His coming,
But in this world of sin,
Where meek souls will receive Him, still
The dear Christ enters in.

O holy Child of Bethlehem!
Descend to us we pray;
Cast out our sin and enter in,
Be born in us today.
We hear the Christmas angels
The great glad tidings tell;
O come to us abide with us,
Our Lord Emmanuel!

—

PHILLIPS BROOKS, 1868

Hark!
The Herald Angels Sing

Hark! the herald angels sing,
"Glory to the newborn King.
Peace on earth and mercy mild;
God and sinners reconciled."
Joyful all ye nations rise.
Join the triumph of the skies;
with angelic host proclaim,
"Christ is born in Bethlehem!"
Hark! The herald angels sing,
"Glory to the newborn King."

—

CHARLES WESLEY, 1739

CHAPTER 8

A Time for
Family and Friends

Christmas is a time for going home. And even when we can't enjoy the physical presence of family and friends, we can still find a special place for them in our hearts.

Christmas is a season when families gather to share food, songs, stories, and memories. Holiday celebrations bring us together, and holiday traditions remind us of our heritage.

This holiday season, like every other, should be a time of thanksgiving and fellowship. And, amid the holiday happenings, let us always remember the One who came to earth so that we might have abundance and salvation. Jesus said, "As the Father loved Me, I also have loved you; abide in My love" (John 15:9 NKJV). He first loved us; let us return His love by sharing it.

Unless the Lord builds a house,
its builders labor over it in vain;
unless the Lord watches over a city,
the watchman stays alert in vain.

Psalm 127:1 HSCB

A new commandment I give to you,
that you love one another;
as I have loved you,
that you also love one another.

John 13:34 NKJV

Now these three remain: faith, hope, and love.
But the greatest of these is love.

1 Corinthians 13:13 HCSB

Christmas is about family:
God's family . . . and yours.

JIM GALLERY

A family is a place where principles are
hammered and honed on the anvil
of everyday living.

CHARLES SWINDOLL

Our homes and families can sometimes
be sources of struggle. But His reality is,
for every family, a source of constant care.
Doesn't that feel good at Christmas?

CALVIN MILLER

89

PETALS OF *Joy*

Apart from religious influence,
the family is the most important
influence on society.

BILLY GRAHAM

✦

The God who adopted you
into His forever family
knows how to make earthly families work.

CHARLES STANLEY

✦

When the family is together on Christmas day,
all is well with the world!

MARIE T. FREEMAN

90

A Christmas family-party!
We know of nothing in nature
more delightful!

CHARLES DICKENS

Christmas is the season of joy,
of holiday greetings exchanged,
of gift-giving, and of families united.

NORMAN VINCENT PEALE

91

Choose for yourselves today
the one you will worship. . . .
As for me and my family,
we will worship the Lord.

—

JOSHUA 24:15 HCSB

CHAPTER 9

A Joyful Season of Prayer

The Christmas season is a time when we offer thanks for Jesus and for the One who sent Him. We express thanksgiving through our words, through our deeds, and through our prayers.

Jesus instructed His followers to pray always, and His advice applies to Christians of every generation. When we weave the habit of prayer into the very fabric of our days, we invite God to become a partner in every aspect of our lives. And, when we make the Christmas season a time of thanksgiving and prayer, we welcome the Christ child into our hearts, which, of course, is exactly where He belongs.

A life growing in its purity and devotion
will be a more prayerful life.

E. M. BOUNDS

Obedience is the master key
to effective prayer.

BILLY GRAHAM

Prayer guards hearts and minds and causes
God to bring peace out of chaos.

BETH MOORE

Two wings are necessary to lift our souls
toward God: prayer and praise.
Prayer asks.
Praise accepts the answer.

MRS. CHARLES E. COWMAN

Find a place to pray where no one imagines
that you are praying.
Then, shut the door and talk to God.

OSWALD CHAMBERS

Prayer connects us with
God's limitless potential.

HENRY BLACKABY

*Keep asking,
and it will be given to you.
Keep searching, and you will find.
Keep knocking,
and the door will be opened to you.
For everyone who asks receives,
and the one who searches finds,
and to the one who knocks,
the door will be opened.*

—

MATTHEW 7:7-8 HCSB

God makes prayer as easy as possible for us.
He's completely approachable and available,
and He'll never mock or upbraid us
for bringing our needs before Him.

SHIRLEY DOBSON

When will we realize that we're not troubling
God with our questions and concerns?
His heart is open to hear us—his touch nearer
than our next thought—as if no one in the world
existed but us. Our very personal God
wants to hear from us personally.

GIGI GRAHAM TCHIVIDJIAN

God will help us become the people
we are meant to be, if only we will ask Him.

HANNAH WHITALL SMITH

And everything—whatever you ask in prayer,
believing—you will receive.

MATTHEW 21:22 HCSB

Rejoice always! Pray constantly.
Give thanks in everything,
for this is God's will for you in Christ Jesus.

1 THESSALONIANS 5:16-18 HCSB

The intense prayer of the righteous
is very powerful.

JAMES 5:16 HCSB

CHAPTER 10

Joyful Christmas Memories

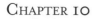

Christmas is a time for memories: revisiting old ones and making new ones. If we're lucky and wise, we do both.

No season carries with it as many reminiscences as the holiday season. As December 25th approaches, we are confronted with a double dose of memory-evoking events: the end of another year and the passing of another Christmas. No wonder we find ourselves reflecting on the past.

This year, as we celebrate this holiday season and give thanks for the ones that have gone before, let us thank God for all His blessings: past, present, and future. And let us keep our happy memories of Christmases past forever in our hearts.

Christmas: that magic blanket that wraps itself
about us, that something so intangible that it is
like a fragrance. It may weave a spell of nostalgia.
Christmas may be a day of feasting, or of prayer, but
always it will be a day of remembrance,
a day in which we think of everything
we have ever loved.

AUGUSTA E. RUNDEL

Happy, happy Christmas, that can win us back
to the delusions of our childhood days,
recall to the old man the pleasures of his youth,
and transport the traveler
back to his own fireside and quiet home!

CHARLES DICKENS

Line by line, moment by moment, special times are
etched into our memories in the permanent ink
of everlasting love in our relationships.

GLORIA GAITHER

Christmas is a good time to take stock
of our blessings.

PAT BOONE

We recall the special Christmases
that are like little landmarks
in a life of a family.

MARJORIE HOLMES

As another Christmas passes,
the memory of it stays and hovers
like the scent of cedar.
And even if it can't be Christmas all the year,
memories remain.

MINNIE PEARL

101

During the Christmas season,
I hope that your own times
of excitement and sharing and
fellowship will leave you
with a special gift—
memories that will last
a lifetime.

—

JAMES DOBSON

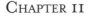

CHAPTER II

Celebrating God's Promises

The words of Matthew 4:4 remind us that, "Man shall not live by bread alone, but by every word that proceeds from the mouth of God" (NKJV). During the season when we celebrate the birth of God's Son, we should study the Bible and meditate upon its meaning for our lives. Otherwise, we deprive ourselves of a priceless gift from our Creator.

God has given us the Holy Bible for the purpose of knowing His promises, His power, His commandments, His wisdom, His love, and His Son. As we study God's teachings and apply them to our lives, we live by the Word that shall never pass away.

God did not write a book and send it by messenger
to be read at a distance by unaided minds.
He spoke a Book and lives in His spoken words,
constantly speaking His words and causing
the power of them to persist across the years.

A. W. TOZER

The most important thing about the Bible
is that it points us to the living Word of God,
which is Jesus Christ.

BILLY GRAHAM

How do you wait upon the Lord?
First you must learn to sit at His feet
and take time to listen to His words.

KAY ARTHUR

*The Holy Scriptures
are our letters from home.*

—

St. Augustine

Weave the unveiling fabric of God's word
through your heart and mind.
It will hold strong,
even if the rest of life unravels.

GIGI GRAHAM TCHIVIDJIAN

God can see clearly no matter
how dark or foggy the night is.
Trust His Word to guide you safely home.

LISA WHELCHEL

As we spend time reading, applying, and obeying
our Bibles, the Spirit of Truth Who is also
the Spirit of Jesus increasingly reveals Jesus to us.

ANNE GRAHAM LOTZ

Heaven and earth will pass away,
but My words will never pass away.

MATTHEW 24:35 HCSB

All Scripture is inspired by God and is profitable for
teaching, for rebuking, for correcting, for training
in righteousness, so that the man of God may be
complete, equipped for every good work.

2 TIMOTHY 3:16-17 HCSB

Your word is a lamp to my feet
and a light to my path.

PSALM 119:105 NKJV

Nobody ever outgrows Scripture;
the book widens and deepens with our years.

C. H. SPURGEON

The Gospel is not so much a demand
as it is an offer, an offer of new life to man
by the grace of God.

E. STANLEY JONES

The only way we can understand the Bible
is by personal contact
with the Living Word.

OSWALD CHAMBERS

The Scriptures were not given for our information,
but for our transformation.

D. L. MOODY

When the child of God looks into
the Word of God, he sees the Son of God.
And, he is transformed by the Spirit of God
to share in the glory of God.

WARREN WIERSBE

The Bible is the cradle
wherein Christ is laid.

MARTIN LUTHER

Words fail to express my love for this holy Book,
my gratitude for its author,
for His love and goodness.
How shall I thank Him for it?

<small>LOTTIE MOON</small>

If you want to know God
as He speaks to you through the Bible,
you should study the Bible daily,
systematically, comprehensively,
devotionally, and prayerfully.

<small>JAMES MONTGOMERY BOICE</small>

*The stars may fall,
but God's promises
will stand and be fulfilled.*

—

J. I. PACKER

The vigor of our spiritual
lives will be in exact
proportion to the place
held by the Bible in our lives
and in our thoughts.

—

GEORGE MUELLER

CHAPTER 12

The Time for Renewal

From time to time, we may find ourselves running on empty, especially at Christmastime. The pressing demands of the holiday season may temporarily rob us of the joy and the peace that might otherwise be ours through Christ.

When the obligations of Christmas drain our strength and test our patience, there is a source from which we can draw the power and the perspective needed to recharge our spiritual batteries. That source is God.

If we genuinely lift our hearts and prayers to our Heavenly Father, He renews our strength. And, when we take time to study God's Word, we are confronted with a profound truth: the challenges of today will soon fade away, but God's love endures forever.

I'm ever and always a stranger to grace.
I need this annual angel visitation to know
the virgin conceives and God is with us.

EUGENE PETERSON

No matter how badly we have failed,
we can always get up and begin again.
Our God is the God of new beginnings.

WARREN WIERSBE

Create in me a clean heart, O God,
and renew a steadfast spirit within me.

PSALM 51:10 NKJV

God is the One who provides our strength,
not only to cope with the demands of the day,
but also to rise above them.
May we look to Him for the strength to soar.

JIM GALLERY

When we spend time with Christ,
He supplies us with strength and encourages us
in the pursuit of His ways.

ELIZABETH GEORGE

A divine strength is given to those
who yield themselves to the Father
and obey what He tells them to do.

WARREN WIERSBE

But those who wait on the Lord
Shall renew their strength;
They shall mount up with wings like eagles,
They shall run and not be weary,
They shall walk and not faint.

<small>Isaiah 40:31 NKJV</small>

Father, for this day, renew within me
the gift of the Holy Spirit.

<small>Andrew Murray</small>

Then He who sat on the throne said,
"Behold, I make all things new."

<small>Revelation 21:5 NKJV</small>

He is the God of wholeness and restoration.

STORMIE OMARTIAN

❧

God specializes in things fresh and firsthand.
His plans for you this year may outshine
those of the past.
He's prepared to fill your days
with reasons to give Him praise.

JONI EARECKSON TADA

❧

Whoever you are, whatever your condition
or circumstance, whatever your past or problem,
Jesus can restore you to wholeness.

ANNE GRAHAM LOTZ

When we invite Jesus
into our lives,
we experience life in the fullest,
most vital sense.

—

CATHERINE MARSHALL

God is great and God is powerful,
but we must invite him to be powerful in our lives.
His strength is always there,
but it's up to us to provide a channel through
which that power can flow.

BILL HYBELS

The amazing thing about Jesus is that
He doesn't just patch up our lives,
He gives us a brand new sheet,
a clean slate to start over, all new.

GLORIA GAITHER

*Therefore if anyone
is in Christ,
he is a new creature;
the old things passed away;
behold, new things have come.*

—

2 Corinthians 5:17 HCSB

CHAPTER 13

Sharing the Joy and Good Cheer

Christmas is the perfect time to share feelings of joy and good cheer. And, of course, the more good feelings we share, the more we have left over for ourselves.

The Christian life is a cause for celebration. Christ promises us a life of abundance, wholeness, and joy, but He does not force His joy upon us. We must claim His promises for ourselves, and when we do, Jesus, in turn, fills our spirits with His power and His love. Then, as God's children, we can share Christ's joy and His message with a world that needs both.

A smile is the light in the window
of your face that tells people you're at home.

BARBARA JOHNSON

Life goes on.
Keep on smiling and the whole world
smiles with you.

DENNIS SWANBERG

122

*A cheerful heart has
a continual feast.*

—

PROVERBS 15:15 HCSB

Christ can put a spring in your step
and a thrill in your heart.
Optimism and cheerfulness are products
of knowing Christ.

BILLY GRAHAM

Christmas began in the heart of God.
It is complete only when it reaches
the heart of man.

ANONYMOUS

When we bring sunshine into the lives of others,
we're warmed by it ourselves.
When we spill a little happiness, it splashes on us.

BARBARA JOHNSON

Make the least of all that goes and the most of all
that comes. Don't regret what is past.
Cherish what you have. Look forward to all that
is to come. And most important of all,
rely moment by moment on Jesus Christ.

GIGI GRAHAM TCHIVIDJIAN

Perhaps the best Yuletide decoration
is being wreathed in smiles.

ANONYMOUS

The Lord reigns; let the earth rejoice.

PSALM 97:1 NKJV

*If you can keep
Christmas for a day,
why not always?*

—

HENRY VAN DYKE

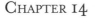

CHAPTER 14

Strength for the Holidays

As December 25th grows closer, we may find ourselves feeling exhausted or worse. The unrelenting demands of the holiday season may temporarily rob us of the joy and the peace that might otherwise be ours through Christ.

When the inevitable pressures of the holiday season sap our strength or test our patience, there is a source from which we can draw the power we need to recharge our spiritual batteries. Our Heavenly Father is that source.

If we genuinely lift our hearts and prayers to God, He renews our strength. Our task, of course, is to let Him.

PETALS OF *Joy*

The same God who empowered Samson,
Gideon, and Paul seeks to empower my life
and your life, because God hasn't changed.

BILL HYBELS

Just as omitting an essential vitamin from
our diet will make us physically weak,
so a lack of prayer will make us spiritually anemic.

BILLY GRAHAM

If we take God's program,
we can have God's power—not otherwise.

E. STANLEY JONES

*Finally, be strengthened by the Lord
and by His vast strength.*

EPHESIANS 6:10 HCSB

*You, therefore, my child,
be strong in the grace that is in Christ Jesus.*

2 TIMOTHY 2:1 HCSB

*The Lord is my strength and my song;
He has become my salvation.*

EXODUS 15:2 HCSB

All the power of God—the same power that hung
the stars in place and put the planets in their
courses and transformed Earth—now resides
in you to energize and strengthen you to become
the person God created you to be.

ANNE GRAHAM LOTZ

No matter how heavy the burden,
daily strength is given, so I expect we need not
give ourselves any concern as to what
the outcome will be.
We must simply go forward.

ANNIE ARMSTRONG

Notice what Jesus had to say concerning those
who have wearied themselves by
trying to do things in their own strength:
"Come to me, all you who labor and
are heavy laden, and I will give you rest."

HENRY BLACKABY AND CLAUDE KING

God's help is always available,
but it is only given to those who seek it.

MAX LUCADO

Our Lord never drew power from Himself,
He drew it always from His Father.

OSWALD CHAMBERS

A mighty fortress is our God,
a bulwark never failing . . .

MARTIN LUTHER

*I raise my eyes toward
the mountains.
Where will my help come from?
My help comes from the Lord,
the Maker of heaven and earth.*

—

PSALM 121:1-2 HCSB

God will never lead you where
His strength cannot keep you.

BARBARA JOHNSON

Measure the size of the obstacles
against the size of God.

BETH MOORE

God's saints in all ages have realized
that God was enough for them.
God is enough for time;
God is enough for eternity.
God is enough!

HANNAH WHITALL SMITH

We have ample evidence that the Lord
is able to guide. The promises cover
every imaginable situation. All we need to do
is to take the hand he stretches out.

ELISABETH ELLIOT

The Lord God of heaven and earth,
the Almighty Creator of all things,
He who holds the universe in His hand as though
it were a very little thing, He is your Shepherd,
and He has charged Himself with the care
and keeping of you, as a shepherd is charged
with the care and keeping of his sheep.

HANNAH WHITALL SMITH

In God's faithfulness lies eternal security.

CORRIE TEN BOOM

CHAPTER 15

Celebrating Christ's Love

The inescapable promise of Christmas is this: Christ loves us. Even though we are imperfect, fallible human beings, and even though we have fallen far short of God's commandments, Christ's love is perfect and steadfast.

On the very first Christmas day, when God sent His Son to become the salvation of the world, He bestowed the ultimate gift, a gift that is beyond price and beyond human comprehension. We have not earned our salvation; even the best among us fall far short of God's commandments. But, when we accept Christ as our Savior, we are saved by God's grace.

As we celebrate His birth, let us accept Christ's love and share His Good News. Christ's love changes everything; may we, as believers, allow it to change everything in us.

We tend to focus our attention at Christmas
on the infancy of Christ.
The greater truth of the holiday is His deity.
More astonishing than a baby in the manger is
the truth that this promised baby is the omnipotent
Creator of the heavens and the earth!

JOHN MACARTHUR

If you come to Christ, you will always have
the option of an ever-present friend.
You don't have to dial long-distance.
He'll be with you every step of the way.

BILL HYBELS

Greater love has no one than this,
than to lay down one's life for his friends.

JOHN 15:13 NKJV

CELEBRATING CHRIST'S LOVE

*The star of Bethlehem
was a star of joy.
"When they saw the star,
they rejoiced with exceedingly
great joy." All true joy
comes from Him.*

D. JAMES KENNEDY

Love came down at Christmas,
Love all lovely,
Love divine;
Love was born at Christmas;
star and angels
gave the sign.

—

CHRISTINA ROSSETTI

I truly believe that if we keep telling
the Christmas story, singing the Christmas songs,
and living the Christmas spirit, we can bring joy
and happiness and peace to this world.

NORMAN VINCENT PEALE

Jesus stooped into an actual identification
with human nature, and, by that stoop,
lifted human nature into the spaciousness
of fellowship with God.

G. CAMPBELL MORGAN

The stunning point of Christmas is that
God considered my needs and the worth
of my relationship to Him to be sufficient cause
to go through the trauma of changing places.

JOE STOWELL

I have come that they may have life,
and that they may have it more abundantly.

John 10:10 NKJV

I have come as a light into the world,
so that everyone who believes in Me
would not remain in darkness.

John 12:46 HCSB

I am the door. If anyone enters by Me,
he will be saved.

John 10:9 NKJV

And remember, I am with you always,
to the end of the age.

Matthew 28:20 HCSB

At the name of Jesus
every knee should bow,
of those in heaven, and of those
on earth, and of those under
the earth, and that every tongue
should confess that
Jesus Christ is Lord,
to the glory of God the Father.

—

PHILIPPIANS 2:10-11 NKJV

A believer comes to Christ;
a disciple follows after Him.

VANCE HAVNER

I have learned that the more we understand
how very much God loves us,
and the more we comprehend the grace
He has demonstrated toward us,
the more humble we become.

SERITA ANN JAKES

A disciple is a follower of Christ.
That means you take on His priorities as your own.
His agenda becomes your agenda.
His mission becomes your mission.

CHARLES STANLEY

Jesus Christ is not a security from storms.
He is perfect security in storms.

KATHY TROCCOLI

Being a Christian is more than
just an instantaneous conversion;
it is like a daily process whereby you grow
to be more and more like Christ.

BILLY GRAHAM

Discipleship means personal,
passionate devotion to a Person,
our Lord Jesus Christ.

OSWALD CHAMBERS

Christ is not valued at all unless
He is valued above all.

ST. AUGUSTINE

Begin to know Him now,
and finish never.

OSWALD CHAMBERS

Jesus:
the proof of God's love.

—

PHILIP YANCEY

A Son of God who defends his title with
the arguments that he is the brother of even
the poorest and the guilty and takes their burden
upon himself, this is a fact one can only note
and shake one's head in unbelief, or one must
worship and adore. There is no other alternative.
I must worship.
That's why I celebrate Christmas.

HELMUT THIELICKE

The simple shepherds heard the voice
of an angel and found their Lamb;
the wise men saw the light of a star
and found their Wisdom.

FULTON SHEEN

Our hope in Christ is the mainstream of our joy.

C. H. SPURGEON

CELEBRATING CHRIST'S LOVE

He loved us not because
we're lovable, but because
He is love.

—

C. S. LEWIS

Everywhere, everywhere
Christmas tonight!
For the Christ child who
comes is the master of all;
No palace too great,
no cottage too small.

—

PHILLIPS BROOKS

*Who can separate us from
the love of Christ?
Can affliction or anguish
or persecution or famine or
nakedness or danger or sword? . . .
No, in all these things we are more
than victorious through
Him who loved us.*

—

ROMANS 8:35, 37 HCSB

149

And they shall call
His name "Immanuel,"
which is translated,
"God with us."

—

MATTHEW 1:23 NKJV

CHAPTER 16

Celebrating the Gift of Eternal Life

Two thousand years ago, God fulfilled His promise by sending His Son into this world so that those who open their hearts to Him might have eternal life. God has made His promise clear: when we accept God's Son and accept God's grace, then we will receive life abundant and eternal. And that, of course, is God's ultimate Christmas gift to the world, a gift of love that is infinite, unshakable, unchanging, and eternal.

It is by God's grace that we have been saved, through faith. We are saved not because of our good deeds but because of our faith in Christ. May we, who have been given so much, praise our Savior for the gift of salvation, and may we share the joyous news of our Master's love and His grace.

PETALS OF *Joy*

For the Son of Man
has come to seek
and to save the lost.

—

LUKE 19:10 HCSB

Teach us to set our hopes on heaven,
to hold firmly to the promise of eternal life,
so that we can withstand the struggles
and storms of this world.

MAX LUCADO

And because we know Christ is alive,
we have hope for the present and hope
for life beyond the grave.

BILLY GRAHAM

God has promised us abundance, peace, and
eternal life. These treasures are ours for the asking;
all we must do is claim them. One of the great
mysteries of life is why on earth do so many of us
wait so very long to lay claim to God's gifts?

MARIE T. FREEMAN

*Jesus said to her, "I am the resurrection and the life.
The one who believes in Me, even if he dies, will live.
Everyone who lives and believes in Me
will never die—ever. Do you believe this?"*

JOHN 11:25-26 HCSB

*I have written these things to you who believe
in the name of the Son of God, so that you
may know that you have eternal life.*

1 JOHN 5:13 HCSB

*Pursue righteousness, godliness, faith, love,
endurance, and gentleness. Fight the good fight
for the faith; take hold of eternal life,
to which you were called and have made
a good confession before many witnesses.*

1 TIMOTHY 6:11-12 HCSB

Amazing Grace!
How sweet the sound
that saved a wretch like me!
I once was lost
but now am found;
was blind, but now I see.

—

JOHN NEWTON

God did not spring forth from eternity;
He brought forth eternity.

C. H. SPURGEON

Slowly and surely, we learn the great secret of life,
which is to know God.

OSWALD CHAMBERS

Once a man is united to God,
how could he not live forever?
Once a man is separated from God,
what can he do but wither and die?

C. S. LEWIS

Christ, the Son of God,
the complete embodiment
of God's Word, came among us.
He looked on humanity's losing
battle with sin and pitched
His divine tent in the middle
of the camp so that
He could dwell among us.

—

BETH MOORE

Grace comes from the heart of a gracious God
who wants to stun you and overwhelm you with
a gift you don't deserve—salvation, adoption,
a spiritual ability to use in kingdom service,
answered prayer, the church, His presence,
His wisdom, His guidance, His love.

BILL HYBELS

O Sovereign God! You have humbled yourself
in order to exalt us. You became poor so that we
might become rich. You came to us so that
we can come to you. You took upon yourself our
humanity in order to raise us up into eternal life.
All this comes through your grace, free and
unmerited; all this through your beloved Son,
our Lord and Savior, Jesus Christ.

KARL BARTH

*I have been all over the world,
and I have never met anyone
who regretted giving
his or her life to Christ.*

—

BILLY GRAHAM

Joy to the world! the Lord is come:
Let earth receive her King;
Let every heart prepare him room,
And heaven and nature sing.
And heaven and nature sing.
And heaven, and heaven,
and nature sing.

—

ISAAC WATTS